WHY BELIEVE IN
MALE/
FEMALE
DIFFERENCES

WHY BELIEVE IN
MALE/
FEMALE
DIFFERENCES

PROFESSOR JENSEN & STUDENTS

WHY BELIEVE IN MALE/FEMALE DIFFERENCES

iUniverse books may be ordered through booksellers or by contacting:

iUniverse
1663 Liberty Drive
Bloomington, IN 47403
www.iuniverse.com
1-800-Authors (1-800-288-4677)

ISBN: 978-1-4917-8171-5 (sc)
ISBN: 978-1-4917-8172-2 (e)

Print information available on the last page.

iUniverse rev. date: 11/19/2015

CONTENTS

Contributors:

Uitilafi Faumuina II
Elissa Greenman
Cody Rogers
Daria Watts
Rainey Whitworth
Yvette Yanes

PREFACE

In our university seminar we investigated how men and women differed one from another. We soon found an enormous amount of research documenting all kinds of differences. It was then that we realized there was a more important question. Why do some academicians want to deny or minimize these important differences between men and women? Soon we realized this was the most interesting question. Why do we want to believe there are gender differences in the first place? We hope you will want to know our answers.

It is our belief that diversity is good; that in this world we are more intelligent when we see distinctions. So it is, when we want to understand gender. Only when we acknowledge and recognize the value of differences or diversity can we fully appreciate our lives and our diverse world. But in any comparison something is contrasted with something else. In this book we want to focus on women as they naturally contrast with men.

It was midway through the semester, after many discussions, the professor decided he could and should write a short clear summary of our answers. Many of the conclusions or insights were first written by the students then reviewed and edited by the professor. You may find them provocative or controversial. In our seminar there were differences of opinion although the majority agrees with what you will now read. We just want to share with you what we have discovered through our reading and discussions.

BELIEVING IN DIVERSITY

Believing in Diversity Leads to Appreciation

A consistent, well-accepted belief among behavioral scientists is that each person is unique. Furthermore, everyone wants to be an individual. Individuality is not only important for understanding differences but is important for feeling appreciated. In this book we focus on differences and believe that this will result in greater appreciation for both men and women. Appreciation is shallow, even impossible, if the person in front of you is considered to be like all others. It then is critical to begin by understanding that each of us is unique, unlike any other.

There is a path to follow in moving from understanding to appreciation of gender differences. We have chosen to understand gender differences by focusing on how women differ from men. This choice has lead us to more interesting research and creative thinking as you will discover reading forward. As mentioned earlier and certainly obvious, we begin by recognizing that women differ from each other.

If women are different from each other than logically they would have to differ from men. How else could it be? For the differences between women logically lead to the conclusion that men and women are even more different because each individual woman would differ from each man in her unique way. It would be foolish to close our eyes to the differences. The differences are important. In the book, <u>Sex Differences</u>, the author explains something very significant:

> *Why write a book about the differences between men and women, rather than one about similarities?... the similarities between the sexes are indeed a reality. But it is an insignificant reality, a sort of background noise devoid of consequence. That is why we have chosen to emphasize the differences here, for they alone carry meaning*[1]

Why Believe in Gender Differences?

Why believe in gender differences? Because it is true. It is easily observable, factual. Besides being true and factual, it is practical. Recognizing differences are useful for understanding being successful, and enjoying human relationships. Being aware of sex differences can lead to better understanding and harmony in all human relationships. Being ignorant of the true and real differences or minimizing those leads to blindness and misunderstandings. In the epilogue of her book, <u>*The Female Brain*</u>, Dr. Brizendine states that the denial of gender differences is particularly harmful for women who need to be better understood. Earlier she says:

> *The fear of discrimination based on difference run deep, and for many years assumptions about sex differences went scientifically unexamined for fear women wouldn't be able to claim equality with men. But pretending that women and men are the same, while doing a disservice to both men and women, ultimately hurts women.*[2]

The differences are, of course, greater in some areas than in others but the differences, even small differences, become important when considered together because they interact with each other. The differences are found in the: brain, hormones, body build, reproductive organs, sexuality, body build, size, strength, emotions, personality, reactions to stress, empathy, nurturance, communication, conflict resolution, children's preferences for play and toys, attachment, bonding, preference for family roles, children, work, thinking, intuition, spirituality, religion, attitudes, values, romance, fidelity and sexuality among others.

Scholarly Books Describing Gender Differences

It is not hard to find many scholarly books confirming that there are many meaningful differences between men and women[3] Some start out as biological sex differences but as a baby matures to adulthood there are in all times and places consistent environmental influences that enlarge the differences between men and women.

Rather than trying to document all these differences, let us present or mention just a few of the most credible of these reference books:

A favorite and even a New York Times best seller is The *Female Brain* and also *The Male Brain* written by a neuro- psychiatrist. One of the most well documented books is *Male and Female: The Evolution of Sex Differences* in its second edition written by Professor David Geary, and published by the American Psychological Association. More than 50 distinguished scholars contributed to another book; *Sex Differences in the Brain* to provide an in depth look at the biological foundations for sex differences. Simon Baron-Cohen is professor of psychology and psychiatry at Cambridge University and in an easy to read book, confirms how males and females differ; especially differing in empathizing and what he calls systemizing.

The theme of the book *Sex Differences* is stated in the first line of the introduction:

> *Women and men are equal, but they differ in almost every way possible;*[4]

A reading of these scholarly books will support the everyday observations of most people that there are sex differences. This in turn supports another goal of this book which is to show how and why it is important to understand women in general and at the same time appreciate an individual woman.

WHAT WOMEN WANT, LIKE AND VALUE

Researching What Women Want

When teaching a gender roles class I embarked on a research project with my students to answer the question of what women really want. We read books written by feminists, reviewed scholarly articles and made a list of desired goals. Later we shortened it during the following two semesters to 29 statements. With some help from colleagues at California State in San Luis Obispo, Purdue, Auburn, and Northern Illinois Universities we administered a survey to their students and found 70 to 80 percent agreement on 29 items. [4] In the next survey we shortened the list to 9 items and administered it to a large sample of 600. We found 80% agreement with all the items across ages, gender, and in different sections of the country. Three of those statements are listed below:

> *Women not only differ in anatomy, physiology and reproductive function, they also differ in preference for what they do, the ways they do things, and the values they hold. The cluster of attitudes, values, mannerisms and personality characteristics associated with being a woman is*

called femininity. Femininity should not be denied, but valued.

Women should receive special social consideration, courtesy, and respect. This includes the protection from abusive, vulgar language, protection in times of life-threatening emergencies, and protection of sexual privacy and modesty. Women need some legal protection and benefits that are different from those men need, such as in the areas of work environment, divorce, or military service.

The meaning of sex has a more personal nature in the world of women. Thus, women benefit from policies which prevent sexual exploitation and harassment. In particular, women have and always will need special protection from forceful sexual exploitation and harassment. Women need special protection from forceful sexual intercourse (rape), which is more than just an act of violence but also is an act which violates a woman's sense of dignity and worth. [5]

What Women Do Not Want

A perplexed professional woman was complaining about her recent experience in a management position. She was expected to perform like the successful male executives in her company. She did her best to do just that. But when she did she was criticized by her peers and subordinates for betraying her gender and being artificial. Her words were, "You just can't win."

This is the dilemma that raises its head when the business community is led to believe that there is no difference between men and women and thus conclude woman should do things just like a man. If her employer and co-workers were to recognize the value of differences between men and women, they could then organize the tasks and adjust the expectations to benefit from the difference.

Rita May Kelly in her book, <u>The Gendered Economy</u>, saw how women were to be assimilated into the male public sphere. She writes,

> *From this assimilationist perspective the question all too often is, 'How can we change the talents, motivations, abilities, and bodies of women to fit existing societal structure and needs?*[6]

The obvious answer is, don't.Those who try believing there is no difference between men and women feed into the mistaken idea of trying to put women into the mold of men.

Instead, the sensible and most profitable way to increase wealth and productivity in the marketplace is to value and build upon male and female differences. While women welcome opportunity and an invitation to belong in the workforce, the thing they do not want is to be masculinized. They do not want to work as men or be as men. They want to be valued with their differences and for their differences. Femininity would not exist if women did not value femininity. Most women do not want to sacrifice their femininity to be successful in the public sphere. Believing there is no difference between men and women seems insulting to most women.

Traits Valued by Women

Androgyny may not be androgyny. Within the popular Bem Androgyny test there is a group of items which are answered similarly or hang together statistically and are called by some researchers', "interpersonal sensitivity", distinguishing them from androgyny. The items or traits are: understanding, gentle, compassionate, soft spoken, sympathetic, yielding, tender, happy, loyal, eager to soothe hurt feelings, cheerful, loves children, sensitive to the needs of others, sincere, affectionate, helpful, warm and reliable.

Our research team wanted to know if this interpersonal sensitivity was associated or preferred by females. We made a survey and administered it to students attending Purdue, Mesa College in Arizona, and Brigham Young University[7]. We found that on a scale of 1-5 females scored higher on self-ratings on all of these adjectives.[8]

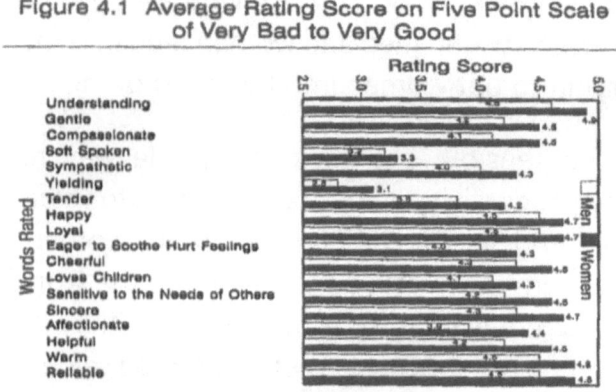

Figure 4.1 Average Rating Score on Five Point Scale of Very Bad to Very Good

Traits Liked By Women Existing in Different Cultures

These same differences between males and females in the traits they feel exist across the cultures of U. S., Korea, China, Thailand We found 8th, 10th, and 12th grades in California, Idaho, New York, and Louisiana differed on liking these traits. The important point is that such gender differences do exist across cultures and surely across time.

Gender differences have always been part of every time and place. Do we want now to eliminate them? Is there a good, or a benefit for preserving or continuing to accept the finding that women report that they value gentleness, compassion, being soft spoken, sympathetic, yielding, tender, happy, loyal, sensitive, helpful, warm, and reliable? For us this truism is self-evident in the private sphere of a women's world, socially and historically.[9]

MEN AND WOMEN AND THE WORLD.

Public Man, Private Women

A highly respected political scientist, Jean Bethke Elshtain, addresses a central concept for understanding the basis of male female differences in her book: Public Man, Private Woman. She identifies the essential element explaining,

> ...most of a woman's traditional concerns, passions, and responsibilities will fall outside the grid of a 'public space.[10]

While she argues for equal male and female participation in the public sphere of government, community, church, schools, work; she clearly identifies women's deeper attachment and felt importance in the private world, or sphere of home and family.

The status of women, the importance of women, the influence of women, the happiness and concern of women is greater in the family than anyplace in the public sphere. Elstain illustrates this with the following words,

Children, however exhibit little doubt that their mothers are powerful and authoritative, though perhaps not in the same ways identical to fathers. This ideal of parental equality does not presuppose sameness between mother and father. Each can be *more or less a private or a public person, yet be equal in relation to children. (p.126)*[11]

> The necessity of seeing the difference between the public and private worlds is important for understanding sex differences. While gender equality should exist in both worlds, it is in the private world where women flourish most naturally to find meaning and value most easily. Thus, appreciation of women is directly proportional to the attention and importance given to the private world.

Do Women Live in a Different World?

Four women scholars suggest an interesting possibility. It is that women have a culture of their own, or more broadly stated: Women live in a different world. From their books we tried to study in more depth this intriguing notion. After reading their books we identified the following characteristics distinguishing the women's world from the men's world:

- Relationship oriented rather than material goals.
- More concerned with good than right.
- Relies more on intuition, less on logical thinking.
- Greater focus on the 'other' rather than the 'self'.
- More emotional.
- Personal development via interaction with others.
- Acquired more through nurturing.
- Acquired more through bonding and attachment.
- More identification with others/family. [12]

How these differences in world view come about is surely complex, but must begin with biological sex differences, and then modified by varying social and cultural beliefs about gender. There are multiple theories about how gender is formed but most include different definitions of boy and girls, activities, standards and expectations. The world comes to be experienced differently by each sex from infancy and even into adulthood.

A causal reading of the above nine differences (and there are more) surely leads one to see a values in both the male and the female world views. The greatest value occurs when the two are combined or balanced together. It is for this reason that the insistence that gender differences be abolished or minimized is a serious mistake. When carefully examined, it is the woman's world that is most seriously compromised or hurt when the woman is asked to conform to the dominant cultural view which is the man's world.

How Women and Men View the World

We read books and articles about differences between men and women. Then with the help of students, a list of 50 at- tributes about which women and men differ was obtained. Were these scholars correct? Rather than speculate we de- cided to do what psychologists are supposed to do. We made a test and students asked two married couples to choose between two word pairs indicating which word they preferred. There were differences between husbands and wives.[16] The percentages indicate liking the words in the first column of the table below.

Is it not easy to see how knowing these differences can lead to greater understanding and more harmonious living with the opposite sex?

	Men	Women
Logic vs. intuition	79%	36%
Power vs. compromise	36%	4%
Character vs. kindness	68%	29%
Consistency vs. forgiveness	64%	32%
Freedom vs. children	32%	7%
Facts vs. feelings	32%	4%
What people do vs. what people like inside	64%	14%
Justice vs. mercy	46%	35%
Enjoy work vs. enjoy people	64%	11%
Determination vs. patience	42%	21%
Achievement vs. getting along with others	54%	18%
Success vs. friends	36%	11%
Competitive ability vs. cooperative ability	25%	0%
Being in charge vs. helping	39%	7%

Women like Family

It is clear that women want and deserve freedom, choices, protection, respect, and opportunities. There is really no argument about this. Barriers to freedom for women are being crushed by public sentiment. Far reaching are laws against gender discrimination. But what women want goes beyond preventing discrimination. In 2012 Madeleine Kunin wrote in her book, _The New Feminist Agenda_, a new realization. It is that past achievements have neglected the core desire and need of women. It is a focus on the family.

She enumerates the great increase in openings of opportunities for female employment and education. She notes that sixty percent of the students at universities are female. She also cites a New York Times article listing advances such as women running for President, women arguing before the Supreme Court, performing heart surgery, fighting for the country, directing movies, flying into space just to note the forward steps that have occurred during the last half of the 20th century. But she states,

> _It may seem a retrograde to suggest that feminists like me, who strove to liberate ourselves from the limited roles of wife and mother, have come full circle to focus, once again, on the family._[17]

CAN YOU WISH GENDER AWAY?

Are Gender Differences Hardwired in the Brain?

While we and other social scientists have reported behavioral, social, and attitudinal differences between men and women, we cannot help but speculate about the cause of gender differences. One answer is that sex differences are hard wired in the brain; here are three credible sources with this conclusion.

Cambridge Professor, Simon Baron-Cohen, [18] says that the female brain is hardwired for empathy and the male brain hardwired for understanding of what he calls "building systems", although he recognizes exceptions. He does report biological differences where women are more inclined to deal with feelings, to reach out socially, and to be emotionally intuitive. He then believes these differences lead them to preferences for different roles and activities than men.

The belief in biologically based social differences is supported in the conclusions of evolutionary biologist David Geary who reports findings that:

> Studies of personal values and interests reveal a consistent pattern of social sex differences, with women more than men, valuing the development of altruistic, reciprocal relationships with other people and men, more than women, being

> *interested primarily in power, competition, and struggle...*[19]

The hardwiring means that there are differences in the brain. But modern neuroscience recognizes it is not just brain anatomy. The brain continually interacts and changes with hormonal influences.

Brain Sexual Differentiation

In the Netherlands Institute for Brain Research located in Amsterdam, researcher D. F. Swaab has been examining the human brain to explore the idea of gender identity as well as sexual orientation.

Swaab explains that sexual differentiation is thought to be imprinted or organized by hormonal signals from the developed male gonads. He continues to explain that this male sex difference of the brain is thought to be determined in the first two periods during gestation and the perinatal period, then to puberty onwards: sex hormones alter the function of previously organized neuronal systems.[20] Testosterone plays such an essential role because both sexes are exposed to high levels of estrogens during the fetal life- while it is only males who are in fact subjected to high an- drogen levels. In conclusion Swaab addresses hormonal differences that impact the brain and as a result of this, dif- ferences are present and play a role in the behavioral differ- ences between men and women.

What is a Minimalist?

While there are many reasons why a person would want to believe in sex differences, there are some who don't. They believe strongly that men and women should be treated as equals, and a belief that there is no difference between men and women, and this belief is valued to support the social/political policies of equality. In other words; if men and women can be shown to be the same then they can be regarded as equal. Thus persons with this belief want to minimize reported differences between men and women.

For example Anne Fausto-Sterling, a minimalist, published the book, <u>Myths of Gender</u> in 1985. She does not want to believe men and women think, believe, or behave differently. It is the most scholarly classic feminist attack on what she believes to be a male biased science. She openly presents scientific research reports showing gender differences and skillfully dismantles each. Her arguments include the following:

1. She shows that small statistical differences in averages are not important.
2. She then shows that the differences found between men and women are small compared to the differences within groups or between women.
3. She continues her attack by showing and exposing methodological weaknesses such as poor selection of subjects or errors of measurement (of which all experiments have some inadequacies.)
4. She also is very skilled in reinterpreting the differences between men and women.

She does not shy away from putting forward her belief that the feminist desire to minimize gender differences is correct. In her words,

> *Put another way, I have framed the issue as poorly done science, while at the same time undertaking to look beyond the existence of good science to something called feminist science.*[21]

She does not like either biomedical science or behavioral approaches because they ignore aspects of women' experience. If one can look past her passion against male bias in science, a great deal can be learned from her extensive review of the literature and research on gender differences.

An Answer to Minimalist Concerns

In an attempt to minimize reported gender differences, minimalists argue that the male/female findings are small, that differences between women and women or men and men reduce the meaningfulness of male/female differences. They also believe the research is of poor quality and the results can be interpreted to minimize the data.

Addressing her objections of research demonstrating gender differences, the following are responses to each of her four points:

1. Many small differences may be as significant as a few large differences. Furthermore, not all of the reported differences are small.
2. It is true that there are within group differences. (Within group differences are the differences between women.) But within group differences does not negate between group differences between men and women. Notice that in life most interactions between men and women take place between one man and one woman. So differences between men and women will be manifest even if there are within group differences between women.
3. The methodological weaknesses in gender difference research could be called sloppy research, but that only increases the variability, which in turn reduces the probability of finding a statistical difference. Thus, the actual conclusion should be that differences between

men and women will more likely be seen and be significant when better research is under-taken.

4. Certainly, alternative explanations are insightful and intelligent but so are interpreting the data to demonstrate male and female differences.

Debating the Magnitude of Gender Differences

To minimize the size of the sex differences that are consistently found across many measures, Janet Hyde collected 46 meta-analyses. Each of these contained many individual reports, which measured effect size or the magnitude of reported gender difference research. The result was that 48% of the effect size was in the small range and an additional 30% were near zero. For her, fully 78% of the effect sizes for gender differences were small or close to zero. [22]

Two years later Marco Del Giudice reanalyzed Hyde's data using a more advanced or sensitive multivariate statistic and found that by including more contributing variables in the statistical analysis large gender differences existed in these studies. He states that the overall size of sex differences in human aggression may be more than twice as large as the average of the univariate estimates of effect size. This applies to other differences as well as the more powerful multivariate statistics will almost invariably produce larger estimates of the statistical distances between the sexes. [23]

The value and importance of this debate impacts theory but also day-to-day practical living. If there are gender differences, they need to be known and intelligently considered. The contrasting argument has been that knowledge of gender differences will be used to subjugate and oppress women. Therefore, it is best to minimize differences to avoid this misuse.

Of course, it is well known that any kind of knowledge can be used for both good and bad. But the solution is not to minimize knowledge but to make every effort to use true knowledge for the benefit of all. So it is with sex differences. A good example of this is Deborah Tanner's book You Just Don't Understand: Men and Women in Conversation. [24] In a most delightful manner she illustrates how to reduce miscommunications and misunderstandings between men and women by understanding differences in how men and women communicate.

At the End of the No Difference Road

Judith Butler in her book Gender Trouble addresses the question of gender. She goes well beyond the usual assertion that gender is created by society and is merely a social construction. [25] She goes on to say that male and female or the actual biological sex is also a social construction. Furthermore, she believes the use and focus on the word *woman* by some feminists and the general society supports the patriarchal binary error of having only a male and female gender.

It is clear that her philosophical theory and review of feminist thought is motivated by what is presented in the last chapters of her book. Her goal is to reconstruct gender in such a way as to have more than just male and female or man and woman.

Her somewhat unique way to accomplish this is to view gender as a performance rather than a set essence, or binary category. For her gender is constantly generated by an individual's performance. She uses the words of, "stylized bodily acts in repetition to produce 'core' gender". The performance of gender is guided by "regulated discourse" and determines which possibilities are socially permitted to be natural in the culture.

Her theory surely goes beyond recognizing gay, lesbian, bisexual, transsexual, and queer by constructing gender as performance. It makes gender meaningless. So then the question is: *"How do we talk about differences if male, female or man and woman do not exist?"*

MAKING THE MOST OF
A GOOD SITUATION

Why Femininity Will Not Go Away

Femininity won't go away because women like it and masculinity won't go away because men like it. Most definitions of femininity include behaviors, feelings, appearances associated with being female as determined by culture. Obviously, culture begins with recognition of differences between male and female and then expands on the biological beginnings. The expansion results in differences between cultures in what is considered masculine and feminine. But a distinction between what is masculine and feminine persists and exists in all cultures. Why? The most obvious explanation of why feminism won't go away is the fact that femininity is chosen or valued by both women and men.

The second reason is that some activities cannot be done or only done with greater difficulty by the other sex; like child bearing or strenuous physical work. In simple terms biological differences between males and females will result in different choices and these choices come to be called masculinity and femininity when they are expanded into beliefs, feelings, and appearances. There will always be differences between cultures in what is considered femininity and these differences will be always changing. But at any one place or time what is regarded as femininity will be valued because it becomes part of a woman's identity. Thus a self-perpetuating phenomenon occurs. A woman's identity as a woman leads to choosing femininity, and choosing femininity creates a stronger gendered identity.

Living with Husband and Wife Differences

Most of us will live the majority of adult life with a member of the opposite sex. We will find that even though there is a great deal of overlap in almost every psychological/biological trait such as physical strength, height, weight, musculature; the pairings of male and female will result in almost every female living with a male who is heavier, stronger, and more physically aggressive.

Thus, many small differences result in some very tangible and real differences for the vast majority of couples. To the woman living with a larger, more muscular and aggressive partner statistical averages seem trivial. This woman, whose numbers constitute a majority, must find a way to address this issue on a day to day basis. The issue is not limited simply to physical aggressiveness. To her, strategies must be developed to satisfactorily live with these and many other differences. The question becomes not whether men and women are biologically different; the question is "Are you different from your spouse?" and the answer almost invariably is "Yes." In these cases, social gender roles come to the assistance of the individual woman. At the individual level, gender roles are viewed much more positively than they are by theorists making a sociological analysis.

Good sex/gender roles can provide protection, security, support, time and justification for status and value in the family. Of course we would not want gender roles that hurt or disadvantage women. When negative gender roles exist the answer is to eliminate them and freely choose to accept and support gender roles women prefer.

Valuing the Differences

Diversity has proven to be a key for the economic and social success of our nation. Our society was built upon diversity in the marketplace, education, government, and even in families. These institutions have been strengthened by accepting, respecting, and profiting from ethnic, class, age, and geographic differences. The male/female differences may prove to be the most pervasive of all diversities in contributing to the vitality and success of society. The value of building upon sex or gender differences may be even more pronounced in the family or home. The critical importance of recognizing gender differences is embedded in the following quote from Alice Rossi in her Presidential Address to the American Sociological Association.

> *Gender differentiation is not simply a function of socialization, capitalist production, or patriarchy. It is grounded in a sex dimorphism. Theories that neglect these characteristics of sex and gender carry a high risk of eventual irrelevance against the mounting evidence of sexual dimorphism from biological neurosciences.*[26]

Now this quote from a noted scholar is directed towards the dangers of ignoring gender differences. But besides avoiding dangers there is the downside of missing opportunities for a greater enjoyment of life when one's gender differences are not respected and valued.

Perhaps C.S. Lewis when discussing the family captures this important direction when he stated the following about domestic work:

> It is surely in reality the most important work in the world. What do ships, railways, mines, cars and governments exist for except that people may be fed warmed and safe in their homes...We wage war in order to have peace, we work in order to have leisure, we produce food in order to eat. So your job is the one for which all others exist.[27]

No Need to Fear Gender Differences

It is important to consider a fear of many feminist scholars. They are reluctant to consider this difference because they feel that if men and women are different, it might somehow justify unequal treatment between the sexes. Addressing this issue, Deborah Tanner states:

> The desire to affirm that women are equal has made some scholars reluctant to show that they are different, because differences can be used to justify unequal treatment and opportunity. Much as I understand and am in sympathy with those who wish there were no differences between men and women only reparable social injustice my research, others' research, and my own and others' experience tell me it simply isn't so.[28]

Enjoying the Differences

So it is difficult to understand the negative motivation behind statements such as:

The long term goal of feminism must be no less than the eradication of gender as an organizing principle of post-industrial society.[29]

The valuing of difference is a step beyond recognizing differences between men and women. The desire to eliminate gender will only lead to frustration for non- believers of male/female differences. Even if a generation could be convinced of no male/female differences, the next generation would wake up to discover the truth that males and females differ. But not only will it be frustrating for those who minimize differences, it will cause them to miss the humor, delight and enjoyment of differences between men and women. Thus this may be the answer we give to the question posed in the title of this book. Why believe in male/female differences?

REFLECTIONS FROM THE AUTHORS

Larry Jensen

It was a pleasure to interact with the other authors during our seminar. We all felt like we were writing about some- thing very important. While we did not always agree the majority opinions are reflected in what we have written. Our goal was to learn while we read and wrote and that was the case for me. I believe we will have a more productive society and each enjoy life more when we appreciate the differences between men and women. Furthermore, I am certain that the long term welfare of women will be better when these differences are acknowledged, valued and re- spected.

Cody Rogers

My first thoughts are that throughout the duration of this class I have indeed been enlightened and have matured in my thinking on the subject of gender differences. This sub- ject has never really crossed my mind before this class and I feel like I had an opinion on it but a very uneducated one. What I found interesting was that mostly all of the class agreed that there were differences between men and women. I was really astonished to see that really no one disagrees with that statement. We are in a time where gender differences are at the forefront if everyone's minds, especially in the Christian Community. Women everywhere are arguing for the right to be equals to men which is something I adamantly agree with. Women should have the same rights, privileges, and opportunities with the same benefits as men. Even though I believe we should be equals instill believe we are different. In discussion with my classmates I learned everyone is equal but as men and women we think differently, even about everyday things. Women are more passionate and caring when they speak. Even in heated debates I don't think I ever heard a woman who come off this way, when all the guys wanted to do was win the argument and if they said something mean, so be it. Now that's not to say there aren't women out there who are like this but the vast majority ardent. I don't know if I have really changed my belief throughout the duration of this class. I'd always known that men and women were different. It was something that had just been obvious to me growing up. Even for my tomboy of a sister who acts more manly than anyone I know. I still can tell that she is a woman. Just by the way she thinks and acts. We are all genetically different. We have different traits that God has given us to make us this way. We have these traits because we have different responsibilities and callings in life. It doesn't make one any better than the other. We are just different.

Yvette Yanes

My first thoughts about the book are that different perceptions have been accounted and that it is on a scholarly basis that all conclusions have been made. I found interesting that the many differences between men and women consist of regular basis interactions and that these interactions have cause psychologist and social scientists to take into depth observations of why and why these are good. I found this important to know because this way I form my own opinions based on informed knowledge instead of mine own observations. Many of our class discussion make me realize that many differences between men women stem from the home and indicate how we form our own recognitions of comparing and contrasting. Professor helped clarify the concept that on a religious stand point men and women aim towards one thing which is to help edify one another in God. My beliefs have not changed about the difference between men and women except has only reemphasized that each man and woman have individual roles. I believe this because societal influences constantly change, enhancing the chances of humankind to continue to develop their own opinions and beliefs.

Daria Watts

At the beginning of this class I did not really understand the big deal with everyone worrying about why men and women are or are not different. I knew what I believed, and how men and women have very distinct differences as a whole, but did not really understand why it was such a controversial issue. After studying and hearing my classmate's opinions, I realized that many people do not believe what I believe. Many do not think there are many differences between the two; men and women. Through researching for this book I have come to see even clearer, there is a difference, along with many similarities. The similarities happen due to the fact we are all human beings. Women are different and similar to each other based on the specific personalities, but that is what makes us human, same as with men. We are not the same person, no one is, but that doesn't mean there is nothing holding us together, like our similarities. I believe that men and women are created in their own way. Each individually, but obviously there is much of a difference in order to have from the beginning of time the labels of man and woman. Men and women are different and similar but on an individual levels. It is important to me to always remember that everyone is different in their own way and have their own beliefs but when it all comes down to it we are similar in the ways that make use human, and we are different in ways that make us individual. I believe that because we have differences we can be better benefits to each other and our societies as a whole.

Rainey Whitworth

While discussing topics in gender and differences, a variety of subjects were examined as well. Individuality we learned is important to feeling appreciated. In the class we learned that by recognizing differences between men and women, both sexes are able to gain a better appreciation for the other. In the book we wrote, arguments are presented as to whether or not there are even differences between the two genders. I think it's important to always remember the variety of ways in which they are different, such as, differences in hormones and the brain itself, different communication styles, and also different conflict resolution styles. Towards the end of our book, we have labeled a chapter "Making the Most of a Good Situation" in which we try and explain to our readers that there will be these differences as you live and come in contact with members of the opposite sex, we try and make sense of the differences and explore possible problems that could arise. Out of all the things I learned throughout this course and by helping to create this unique book, I feel the most important is to know that these differences found in men and women are God given and are a beautiful thing. Men and women are placed on this earth for all individual purposes but also to complement and be able to work alongside with the other.

Elissa Greenman

Growing up in an Christian family, I understood from a young age the different roles that men and women carry. At age 18 however, I had the opportunity to move to Paris France where I saw society in a completely different light; many people do not see the difference between gender roles. For several months as I traveled across Europe I ex- plored the idea and even imagined that, aside from the bio- logical contrast, there may not be a difference between men and women. With this view that I adopted from my new surroundings, I observed many working men and women as well as several stay at home moms to prove my childhood views on gender were wrong. However hard I tried to prove it wrong, I repeatedly found that women and men do re- spond differently to emotions and surroundings- from the corporate man and woman, to male and female surgeon or teacher, every individual acts differently, but I found more similarities with woman and woman/man and man than I found with woman/man. This proves to me that even in a society that dislikes labels, you can't quite escape them. An Oreo cookie is called and Oreo, because that is what it was made to be. A chocolate chip cookie is labeled so because that is what it was intended to be. Despite the different la- bel, both cookies taste great dipped in milk, and some Ore- os are lighter like chocolate chips, while some chocolate chip cookies are crunchier like an Oreo. While the gender label should not define or restrict individuals, it should not be redefined by society simply to accommodate women who relate more to men (and vice versa) I do believe that gender roles exist and that to respect the differences, we can find a more pure equality that comes from different men and women working together.

Uitilafi Faumuina

I think the biggest thing for myself that I have come to real- ize is that the differences are much more complicated than I expected. My initial thoughts were that yes there are many differences between men and women but didn't actually try to take the time to figure what they were. What I have found interesting is hearing both sides of the question and having to put my opinions aside. To read and hear what our class has found and come up with is mind blowing. Not only do the physical side of things play a part in the differences, but also the way the mind thinks, how we act in social situations, the different way we handle stress etc.. With class discussions, Professor Jensen's lectures and all the assignments and research, my views are the same, I'm just less naïve to the fact of how many differences there really are!

Janet Rae Jensen

As a woman, I've thought for many years about gender roles, male/female differences, and the vital influence both genders have in shaping family relations; beginning with the fundamental family unit of marriage between a man and a woman. As my husband, Larry C. Jensen, has researched and taught extensively in this area; I have been at his side listening, learning, and applying, as we have journeyed to- gether for thirty six years.

It has been my privilege to assist him in this Gender Roles Seminar along with several choice university students of varying backgrounds and experiences. This little book has barely touched the surface of a complex and interesting topic that filters through every aspect of life. I look for- ward to future studies and learning more about men and women, our differences and how they complement and weave a pattern through the historical fabric of mankind. And so my "seasoned" journey has only just begun?

END NOTES

1. Christen, Y. (1991) *Sex Differences*, Transaction Pub., London. p. 5.

2. Brizendine, Lou Ann, (2006) *The Female Brain*, Three Rivers Press. N.Y., N.Y. p. 16

3. Christen, Y. (1991) *Sex Differences*, Transaction Pub., London. p. 1

4. Jensen, L. & Christensen, R. (1994*). Finding agreement among women on gender issues*. Psycho- logical Reports, pp. 75, 35-44.

5. Jensen, L., Jensen, J., (1994) *Family Feminism*, Detwelig Enterprises, Calgary, Canada.

6. Kelly, R. M. (1991) *The Gendered Economy*. New- bury Park, California: Sage, pp. 24-25

7. Stimpson, D. Neff, W. and Jensen, L. (1991) *The Caring Morality*; Gender Differences Psychological Reports (69) pp.407-414

8. Jensen, L. and Graft, R. (1991) *Age and Gender Differences in Value Orientation Among Adolescents* (Thesis. Psychology Department, Brigham Young University.

9. Stimpson, D. Neff, W. and Jensen, L. (1992*) Cross Cultural Differences in Preference for a Caring Morality*. Journal of Cross Cultural Psychology

10. Elshtain, J. B. (1981) *Public Man Private Woman*. New Jersey. Princeton University Press, pp. 348-351.

11. Elshtain, J. B. (1981) *Public Man Private Woman*. New Jersey. Princeton University Press, p 126.

12. Bernard, J. (1981) *The Female World.* New York: Free Press

13. Noddings, N. (1984). *Caring :A Feminine Ap- proach to Ethics and Moral Education.* Berkeley, Cal: (1986) University of California Press

14. Baker, J. *A New Psychology of Women.* (1993) Bea- con Press, Boston

15. Gilligan, C. *In a Different Voice.* Harvard Universi- ty Press. Mass.

16. Jensen, L. C. McGhie, A. P. & Jensen, J. R. (1991) *Do Men's and Women's World View Differ?* Psy- chological Reports, 68, pp. 312-314.

17. Kunin, M., (2012) *The New Feminist Agenda,* Chelsea Green Publishing, White River, Ut.

18. Baron-Cohen, S (2003). *The Essential Difference: The truth about the male and female brain.* New York: Basic Books.

19. Geary, D. C. (2010). *Male, female: The Evolution of Human Sex Differences, Second Edition.* Washing- ton, DC: American Psychological Association.

20. Swaab D. F. (2004.) *Sexual differentiation of the human brain: relevance for gender identity, transexualism and sexual orientation.* Gynecol Endocrinal 2004;19: pp. 301–312.

21. Fausto-Sterling, A. *Myths of Gender* (1985) Basic Books, N.Y., N.Y. p. 208.

22. Hyde, J. S. (2007) *New Directions in the Study of Gender Similarities and Differences,* Current Directions in Psychological Science, Vol. 16, pp. 259-263

23. Giudice, M.D. (2009) *The Real Magnitude of Psychological Sex Differences,* Evolutionary Psycholo- gy, vol. 7, pp. 264-279

24. Tanner, D. (2000) *You Just Don't Understand: Men and Women in Conversation* Ballintine, N.Y.

25. Butler, J. (1990) *Gender Trouble,* Routledge Pub- lishing, N.Y., N.Y.

26. Rossi, A. (1985). *Gender and the Life Course.* NewYork: Aldine Publishing Company. p. 161.

27. As cited in Smith, B. (1984) *The Love That Never Faileth,* Bookcraft. Salt Lake City (Letters to C.S. Lewis) Warren H. Lewis, Ed. London: Geoffrey Bles Ltd. 1956. p. 62

28. Tanner, D. (1990) *You Just Don't Understand,* Mor- row Publishing, N.Y., N.Y.

29. Lorber and Ferrell, (eds) 1991 *The Social Construc- tion of Gender Development,* Sage New Berry Park. p. 355

www.ingramcontent.com/pod-product-compliance
Lightning Source LLC
Chambersburg PA
CBHW030544290526
45786CB00004B/1862